Love Songs and Heartbreak Lullabies

Poetry

A. KAY POWELL

ISBN: 1501085727
ISBN 13: 9781501085727

For the Sun and Moon Above.
For Mother and Sister,
with Endless Love.

And now I can truly see,
that if my heart was
broken for any reason,
it was only to write poetry.

Table of Contents

Diamonds

For a diamond
deep within a mountain,
life is rough…
when no one knows
that you are there
looking up.

No one will find you
for years to come,
and thus, the jewel
remains thoughtless.
The glistening goes undone,
there, within the darkness…

while you crave the light.
It is where you can shimmer
and truly come to life
with a fresh start.

To be placed
around a neck
or better yet,

a heart.

Do Not Fall Asleep

Without paddle
or a boat
he thinks he can drift alone.

A sense of direction
he's without,
so, where will he go?

Oh, he's just reaping
what he's sown
for forgetting
what he's known.

And now he's caught
by the sea.
Can you see him—
swimming above the deep?
Tired.
Thirsty.
About to fall asleep.

Tomorrow is Already Today

Tomorrow, tomorrow
we always say.
Tomorrow starts everything,
but tomorrow's already today.

This is a song for the things
that we need to explore.
Forgive us Time,
sweet Time,
we will waste you no more.

Bright light, bright light,
please keep shining.
Why falter now—
we must
keep climbing.

You can never be alone,
please do not cry.
The Holy Spirit is a guide.

Look to self
for that golden
armored butterfly.

If there's nothing left for you,
please feel free
to abide in eternal wisdom.
You can be a king or queen
on your own,
or a slave
in someone else's kingdom.

Tomorrow, tomorrow
we always say.
Tomorrow starts everything,
but tomorrow's already today.

Sweet Sapphire Blue
(there's only you)

Small, we are, within the
vastness of what is true.
But we are the Sun's jewel,
my Sweet Sapphire Blue.

You are such a sight to marvel at.
How can you simply be
a living suspended marble that
gives to all for free
of your blue, brown and green?

Without you, we'd all be helpless.
Sweet Blue:
She's a nurse to all
and yet
she's friendless.
Tried and true,

Sweet Blue:
She knows not money,
but her purse is endless.

How cruel we've been to you.
We're such oblivious screw ups…
looking for God,
while destroying the
most precious gift to us.
We've harnessed wealth at a fast pace.
All the while forgetting
that which made
us wealthy in the first place.

Look how we take from near and far.
Look how we endanger
your beauty with filth—
yet, look how you provide for us still,
like the children that we are—
so, Mother,
forgives us if you will.
Your children are crazy,
shady and sometimes lazy,
but you're all we know.
Without you,
how would we grow?

She has a shield for the sky.
She's a delight to heavenly eyes.
Every day and night
they watch you bloom.
What a paradise
you must look like
to the sun and moon.

How strong you are.
Even after all this hurt
you are still beautiful.
Forgive us, sweet Mother
for not loving you
the way we should…
because

My sweet Sapphire Blue—
you are the rarest of jewels.
My sweet Sapphire Blue—
there is only you.

Words

Words are passing heartbeats
stolen from time,
to live on forever within hearts
and minds.

We must be careful
of words sent with hurt.
They usually come back
with Karma's kiss
and a bit of devil's dirt.

But when we send
freely and often,
words of strength,
hope, and love,
then these three
surrounds us
like invisible doves.

Good Use

Live fully.
Love fully.
For what is now full
shall inevitably
become empty.

But fear not,
for there's
absolute
abundance
everywhere.

And fear not,
for in truth,
all good things
must be put to good use.

Sweet Nectar (The Battle Between Love and Wisdom)

In a golden era, long past,
it is a time of great art,
celebration and rest;
Where children are
born into love,
and raised on
summers of happiness.
Before the Caesars.
Before organized religion.
When man had three lines of vision.

By means
of an unseen portal,
we are now here
within the midst of
two immortals.

These immortals,
they've lived forever…
both needed truly
in equal measure.
One is Beauty.
One is Knowledge.
Both are treasures.
But while Beauty
seeks only pleasure,
in all endeavors,
Knowledge seeks
only understanding
as a large umbrella.

Beauty, she brushes
her beautiful hair
while sitting on her
golden throne:
Her golden vanity,
where she feels at home.

But she is not alone
within this palace—
she feels her sister coming her way—
Her mouth, a golden chalice,
fully equipped with words to say.

Because last night, Aphrodite,
she changed skins,
and as a young maiden
she conquered a prince.

Rolled
eyes.
Look, no surprise.
Here comes Athena,
begging her to be wise

Athena:

> *I never trust lustful men.*
> *They never think more than five minutes ahead.*
> *You silly beauty!*
> *which one of them is your friend?*

Aphrodite:

> Sweet Sister, you trust no one.
> It's the very same reason you're lonesome.

Save your pessimistic rumble of woes.
As far as friends, I am in need of none of those.
I do good or bad on my own,
and I mend my troubles with
logic and productivity.
I am a Goddess you know?

Athena:

> *As am I,*
> *but you're as a child*
> *with an amazing ability to exude a certain*
> *Intelligence—*
> *all irrelevant after two glasses—*
> *in human form you lose your power,*
> *and these indeed...*

Aphrodite:

> ...Are the happiest of hours.

Athena:

> *Yes, when sweet grapes become sour.*
> *Do you realize that,*
> *it's imperative to be wise,*
> *even while you're young?*

Aphrodite:

> I do agree with all my heart's gladness,
> and whatever wisdom I have
> I shall use it to my advantage.
> Like before the day is done,
> I'll have my share of merriments
> under the moon
> right after the sun.

Athena:

> *Indeed, passions will arise,*
> *as what comes with joy*
> *and laughter;*
> *I know how you love to fall in love.*
> *But what about the tears you must dry after*
> *when the falling out of love surely comes.*

Aphrodite:

> My sister, my dear,
> I am no friend of fear.
> I'll be contented within my sadness,
> since tears of love taste sweet like nectar.
> All my battles will have songs,
> and it is there, where love and wisdom meet,
> becoming the victors.

Athena:

> *Yes, to learn all the better.*
> *It's so sad to be silly,*
> *much better to be clever.*
>
> *Yet I'll say that it still doesn't matter:*
> *this 'wisdom of the end',*
> *you should never again mix nectar with them.*
> *Then again—*
> *and I say this shaking my head—*
> *I think maybe you will.*

Aphrodite:

> I think maybe I shall,
> for the fulfillments of all
> existence is what I desire to have.

Athena:
　And this includes?

Aphrodite*:*
　　"Beautiful shoes.
　　Seeing myself in all things.
　　Watching lovers smile
　　as I help them fall in love in the spring.
　　Constant vacations to lands of new.
　　Chats with Father beside
　　the enlightened moon.
　　Taming Ares in June
　　and bathing in the sun.
　　Truly, I simply love
　　Love and Beauty.
　　The gathering of wisdom
　　and understanding is how you have fun;
　　with your scrolls and legends.
　　But you, sweet sister,
　　have never made love in the clouds
　　and looked up at the heavens...
　　Nothing is as sweet,
　　except maybe
　　the sound of the breeze
　　making love to the leaves.
　　All these
　　put my Olympian
　　mind at ease.

　　I know that
　　I have it all already—
　　I am indeed
　　very merry—
　　no need to mingle with them.

But it all gets so
much better when
the nectar goes to my head.
These mortals, they worship me,
so being in their presence
is a Queenly courtesy.

Athena:

We only exist because they do.
You've grown into arrogance,
what is wrong with you?
You're neither proud nor rude;
Like me you're only here to help.
Yet, here you are, my sweet sister,
only helping yourself.

Aphrodite:

"These mortals, they worship me.
Being in their presence
is a Queenly courtesy.

Athena:

There is another side, however, to it all…
One where the lights are blinding,
even to you, the Goddess that you are.
Yea, you play the conqueror of princes, princesses and kings. But
there are cycles to all things.
Soon, they will ransom love for the clarity wisdom
brings.

Inner Life, Outer World

All I have are my dreams.
Easy it seems
in this internal life,
filled with he, me,
love and light.

Now I know it's just a dream,
yet what is life but
a dream you can't escape?
A game with hidden rules,
and fates,
and destinies filled with
mysteries and cake.

Silly you.
You keep dreaming
their dreams and
believing their lies,
that the outer world has more
meaning than your inner life.

Dreams for Two

I know you not
but I am one with you.
I had a dream about you last night.
Come back to me tonight
so that we may continue.

We were in the kitchen
cooking something,
and we were laughing
and we were kissing,
and we were in love.

So much so, that even when I woke up
your love was still there,
still in the air,
and so naturally I ran to the kitchen.

Silly me.
My wishes slip into my dreams.
In real life this love is missing,
so it lingers forevermore...
or so it seems.

But because these dreams
can be sweet,
much sweeter than real life,
come back to me
my sweet,
once more
tonight.

Providence

I guess this is a mercy
and a bit of Providence too,
how you're so used
to your beauty
that you have no clue.

Begging for attention,
beautiful things won't.
They take it,
and if you embrace it,
they'll leave a bit of that
beautiful residue on you,
and you'll be even more beautiful
for the appreciation shown.

As the sun shines
and the wind blows,
flowers have nothing
else to do but grow.

You over there
with eyes to see
and ears to hear,
it's only to you
true beauty can compare.

Yes, it's a mercy
and a bit of Providence too,
how the lake's reflection is
no one else but you.

Hands and Tools

Because every girl needs a prince
and every man needs a fool,
we all play a role
as hand or tool.

If for survival or for fun,
be strong and play along.
Make your bets.
Pay your debts.
Before long,
there'll be nothing left…

All tricks will be finished.
All markets will be
closed for business,
then to each life,
both an angel and a demon
shall be a witness.

Play your part
within this game
or stay away
if you're afraid.

Understand
either way,
it's all a masquerade.
Because every girl needs a prince
and every man needs a fool,
we all play a role
as hand or tool.

Sweet Talk

Of words with wings:
late night
sweet talk is
such a charming thing.

Dare to dream,
sweet queen,
of a king.

Little butterflies feel like birds.
The river flows,
and so it goes…
the desire for more than words.

Wake me up from this living sleep
of wanting no one else.
Now I see
how to keep these living
dreams to myself.

Divine Woe

This Divine Woe
is all that I know.
It is my gift
It is my curse:
how happiness comes
then happiness goes
and I am left
with these verses.

Yes, it is all I know:
lessons that leave
me with treasures
that glow.
But it fits me so,
let it my burden and
my divine woe.
It could all be so much worse
without this strange gift,
and this wonderful curse.

Kites

My lover and I,
we know how
kites get.
Hardly asleep,
we dream.
And here we are...
we breathe out the
weight of the world.

He tells me that he loves me
and I, a humble girl,
tell him to
let me cry for this happiness.
But he's much wiser than I,
so, he tells me to
smile for this God-given thing.
The lasting of which
is up to us first.

And so we kiss
as we lay on God's green sea,
connecting Heaven and Earth.

Life and living is a personal
and on-going friendship
or battle between Man
and his immortal spirit.
But sweet goodness sings
to me of love
and the overcoming of pain.
How do kites get?
We fly higher still,
passed satellites
and constellations
while worrying not for
mundane things.

And we talked.
We talked for hours
about life and love,
the body, the mind
and the powers therein.
We talked about
the immortal spirit,
this planet
and the clarity
of this visit.
The sadness,
the lessons,
the blessings
to be here in
this moment,
this year,

this day,
this very second
on Sapphire Blue...
who has provided us
with all things,
as she is wise and true.

And if it's all a
perfect accident,
then that makes us all,
the entirety of us,
all accidental pieces of art.
And maybe that
should be understandable
and good enough
to give as much compassion
as rightly possible.

The Wind

The wind outside is scary.
It shakes the trees
down to their roots.
The wind outside is scary.
It makes the weary
hooker cry
for more sensible boots.

The wind at the
heart of winter's cold
tends to hold.
It reminds me of all
the uncertainties
and probabilities
that will unfold.

The wind outside is brutal,
but I accept you with a smile.
You are a part of

the endless current of life—
resistance is
absolutely futile.

Sleeping remains the song of spring.
All the animals will try to hide
under their skin.
But the winds of winter are here,
and this, too, must be lived.

I listen well
to hear the greatest stories
never told.
Please continue to sing to me
of the infinite uncertainties
and probabilities that will unfold.

Here and There

The sky is blue,
the grass is green.
The sun shines
through the trees
and a crescent moon
can be seen,
even in the daylight
of a poet's dream.

Birds sing.
Wind blows.
Earth is
in love with us
but only she knows.

Blissful days,
they lay looking up.
Big Sister,
searching for answers
about life and love:

Big Sister:
Is there a man alive
who has had and then
forsaken the lustful times;
who would like to take a trip
within the kiss of love's design?

Little sister:
Possibly so.
I have no worries of such things though.
But I do love a good story,
only if promise not to bore me.

Big Sister:
If I ever find him,
I'll be very kind to him.
We'll go to a place only we know,
forgetting the world
and the sadness it shows.
We'll turn their lead into gold...
The sun and the moon
reflecting the whole.

Little Sister:
Sun and Moon.
King and Queen.
Bride and Groom.
This is fair and just
and oh, so lovely.
Is he here, breathing
the same air as us?
He must be!

Big Sister:
Or maybe he's not.
God likes this type of poetry a lot,
where I'm here and he's there.
We were probably two stars
side by side, at first.
Before we fell to earth.
Before we were
separated by space
and time
and birth.
My twin soul,
will we grow old
and never meet?
Do you like this
type of poetry too?
A lovely mix
of sad and sweet!

While apart,
I hear you like a song
I can't forget.
The melody has the
remnants of a best friend
who was there from the start
as friend and lover.
And we'll be together again,
whether in this life
or another.

The Wheel

Father, Mother, Nurse,
for what you've done
let me thank you first.
Happiness will fill my youth…
but for now,
let's converse on what is true.
What was first here, free and naked,
has all just disappeared.
And what is new has no clue
of what was once sacred.
What was stolen
has long been forgotten.
What was once fresh
is now old and rotten.
Still, all things will
come back into style.
We all simply
must wait a while.
And this is growth, is it not? —
Done only by the living.
It's all in the wheel of life.

Many times, we see adversity as bad, but is it?
Since there's no upward
movement without strife,
and we search for truth
only when we know we're told lies.
The fools will cry
but the sages will smile,
because they already
know of this wheel
and how it offers a wild ride…
with happiness and love
hidden therein to find.

This wheel:
it stretches from the lowest of lows
to the highest of highs.
And it never stops.
Everyone must learn to fly.

On Again

"Look what you've done!
The seas have now become rough.
It was smooth sailing before,
and while it's too soon to tell
if this will be a sad story told,
or something better,
something more pure…
I realize that I'm a mystic
who enjoys sailing alone."

"No one sails alone.
The ride isn't always lovely
but every heart needs a home.
Take the good and the work that I arrive with.
I'm your sun for the darkest days—
a shield for the harshest climates."

"And a lover of all the
pretty flowers that grow—
I prayed that you might let me go,"
"But why, when I love you so,"
"You love us all!"
"That I do,"
"You're such an ass,"
"I love you too.
In fact, I love you more."
"But how is that possible?"

"Have you not heard
of how love is irrational?

"This feels like a riddle.
I am stuck somewhere
in the middle…
where do we go from here?"

He turns to her and says:
"Why, to your lovely
flowerbed my dear.
Your heart has a home."

He kisses her
then laughs,
"I'll never be able to
just let you sail alone."

"Fine, but it has to be
smooth sailing please,
like upon Aphrodite's
gentle breeze."

But he laughed a laugh
for which she found
nothing to compare it.
It passed, he then said:

"You *do* know that your
smooth sailor loved Ares,
his battle ship and their baby.
He was a champion.
She was a beauty.
What else should we do
but love each other truly?"

"But Eros just
represents lust."

"And what else starts
the crazy process of love?"

"It can't be that,
it just can't be."

"Perception builds
the world, entirely.

Now relax and
let the sadness go.
Why in the world would I
let you sail alone?"

Logos

But it isn't
the wind.
It's the thing that
tells the wind where to go.

And It
isn't the sun.
It's the thing that gives
him the authority to glow.

That thing
which is both
near and far,
is the same
thing that starts the beat
to every heart.

It lingers
outside and within.
Only with closed eyes
do we see
we are a part of that thing

That thing is an artist
and scientist
all in one.
That thing is all the things
we hope to become.

No, it isn't the wind
and it isn't the sun,
though it gives power to these,
for the nourishment of
everything and everyone.

Reason

I only lose myself
when it's missing,
so I keep it with me
every day, every minute.

It is sacred.
It is needed.
It is my constant
companion:
Reason.

It allows the knowing
of all notions.
It moves through the world
like a submarine in the deep
blue ocean,
finding treasures
to carry along with it...
navigating, protecting
from pressure, those
who would dwell in it.

Low Key

Up so late
that the dusk meets the dawn
and they both laugh
at how lame I am.

Ok …
Lame?
It couldn't be…
No, not so much.
And why all the fuss,
he's just a man, isn't he?

My thoughts stumbled
and ran away to find peace.
I find myself empty
and have now come upon
the perfect solution
to this tragedy…

Because what can you do
with a heart so broken?

I shall never fall in love,
it's such a crazy game—
I want it gone.
I'll refrain from all
the fuss and madness,
and never again will I stay up
so late with sadness
that the dusk meets the dawn.

A new serenity I've found
as both the dusk and the dawn
take a yawn at me...
watching me, as I
stay away from love
and the maddening crowd that
once surrounded me.

The Wise Men

Yes, Love is a crazy game.
The Wise Men will try to refrain
while pretty fools
are always in love with a lie.

Love is never as it seems.
Sometimes it's better off in dreams.
There, it can never really die.

We were in love for a moment
but then love became hopeless.

At least we dared to try.

I sigh.
It's simply sad.
Love remains the most elusive
and sought after
thing of sea and land.

I sigh.
Love is a crazy game.
The Wise Men try to refrain,
and, unfortunately, so will I.

But still
I sigh at this—
it comes and goes with the seasons.
Even the Wise Men sigh at this
silly romantic treason.
Because a life without love
is a life without meaning.

Romance

Romance is just
Roman antics.
We're all from Rome,
living to know
and devour this loveliness.

Cupid is Caesar,
but Caesar is dead…
no, he's a salad…it's greens…

Romance is just
nourishment
from dreams—
destined to decay at our feet.
Unless we eat,
and acquire its loveliness,
whole and complete.

The Fraternity of Love

Say, it's good to be silly a bit,
if in the end you understand
the riddle of it.

Nature knows no misery…
That, comes from the heart of man.
We judge each other consistently
while our own complexities
we fail to understand.

Sing me a song
that will endure,
of how love is a divergent
and a reoccurring
dream to explore.
Nature makes it so,
therefore, we dream
and dream some more.

For your broken heart,
don't blame the boys—
they were wired this way.
All the world is a toy.
Love is a game to be played.

If we are flowers
then they are bees.
They were meant to fly
and to buzz as they please.

If we are singers
then they like to hear us sing.
It's all a sweet tune
to feel the harmony we bring.

They're so lovely when we're in love.
And we love them still,
even after lessons that leave us
like broken doves on window sills.

It's misery.
It's ecstasy.
It's bliss turned to dust.
It's just chemistry.
It's destiny.
It's the fraternity of love.
It's our birthright to have this
feeling of love and sadness.
Such sweet madness gives meaning to life,
before its bliss turns to dust.

It's just chemistry.
It's destiny.
It's the fraternity of love.

Love is our teacher
and she's so precious,
we can never neglect her.
In the spring
we spend endless hours
watching the bee
come back to his favorite flower.

Indeed,
it's the nectar.

Love:
We never mind the pain that it offers.
Love:
She remains the most highly sought after.

Not even the wise know her secrets.
We fools, we learn as much as we can bear.
The cowards will learn to lose fear.
And kings will lose themselves
or find meaning in all that is dear.

One Place

You're not going to please
anyone
in this world.
Sometimes
you might even
find it hard to please
yourself.

So what's a girl or boy to do
in order to
save face and
conquer fear?

Gather all the
knowledge you've gained
into one place
and go from there.

Whatever You're Into

Love is like the wind—
It comes and it goes.
You may want love
to stay static,
but love is dynamic—
expanding
is all it knows.

Love is like a flower—
beautifully it will grow.
Or jealousy can make it
the weed that eventually chokes.
Love can show
you the way like a
guiding light,
or your puppy love
can turn into a dog fight.

Love will show itself inevitably.
Love is many things.

Love is anything...
We want it to be.

It's molecules and chemicals
constantly shouting.
It's faith that can truly move mountains.
It's a mother's precious love and
a father's protective arms.
On cold days isn't love the sun's warmth?

Love is welcomed
at anytime.
Love is
good food,
good books.
good friends,
and exceptional wine.

Love is the cool
wind of a humid night.
Love is sweet kisses
under the moonlight.
Love is me
writing this corny poem.
Love is paying your friends
back when you owe them.

Love is never as it seems.
It is boundless...always giving,
like rivers to the sea.
Love is as elusive as time can be,
but is still divine.
It is imaginary yet real.
Silly and yet sublime.
Love is the dog

that always comes back.
How easy it is to say.
But love is also pain,
and who wants that?

But want is different
from need.
Pain is the earth
where you plant your
success seeds.
The rain, too, is needed.
The sun always comes back…
So life is complete and
this type of farming
is a true treasure.
The bounty of which
can last one forever.
Love is a warm quilt.
But love also produces a pain
that is crucial.
Without it, nothing gets built
and no one gains anything useful.
Love is a mystery,
but it's oh so simple.
Love is simply
whatever
you're into.

Sheep Puts on a Wolf Coat

While navigating this world alone,
within a vessel made of muscle,
skin and bones,
we'll encounter situations
that require meditation.
Sometimes we'll have to dive deep.

We dive deep into the sky
for inspiration,
and this is where
we find Sheep.

Blissfully,
Sheep lives in grace.
Down there, she's
somewhat out of place.
But with the Creator's fingerprint
stamped on her face,
it was easy being Sheep,
but better being brave.

Sheep smiles as
the sun shines her way.
So very easy on the eyes,
she even loves it when it rains.

Her spirit crafted her character—
a seed from a distant galaxy—
you must wonder how she survives today
and every day thereafter;
among the wolves with
their insidious laughter.

Blissfully Sheep,
she knows she's too sweet…
but it's all in her nature.
If she goes against this,
she betrays her Creator.

So, every day she mirrors
the love back to its source.
And every day is a
blessing of course.
She finds the Creative
in all things given.
Even, simply, in
the art of living.

Because Sheep knows
that in order to win,
a lamb existing among wolves
should put herself in their skin.
So, she's as wolf-like as can be,
watching the real wolves
dressed as she.

What does it matter anyway?

Hearts are broken every day.
The guilty somehow
throw the most stones
and still there
are countless other things to know
while navigating this world alone.

So, she's as wolf-like as can be,
watching the real wolves
dressed as she.

While It Went (a break-up song)

Thanks for the memories you fall out boy.
You were supposed to rescue me,
you were the one who called out joy…
saying how you could give me more.
But you left me to see
that it was never coming to be,
now I'm worse off than I was before.

I must smile at this game,
I'm not the only one.
This journey of love has always been the same…
they say nothing is new under the sun.
Nothing is a mess as you'd perceive.
In fact, maybe it all is
as it should be.

I have more understanding these days—
thank the heavens—
and I never mind the games people play,
or their pretending.
And I'll never mind your reign over my heart.
I was young and in love.
Now, hopefully I will
forget you within this song.

You gave me what I needed:
My sweet lovely self.
So, thanks for the memories…
with your noble, yet, cowardly chivalry.
It was all good while it went.

Angels

Stripped of flight.
No more light.
No more trips to heaven.
Fallen,
broken,
in need of insight...

until they have grown to see
that beautiful
sweet angels
aren't all innocent.

Indeed,
some fight wars too.
Some build up walls,
and who's
free from sin these days?

Not even Angels.

The Creative Mind

I come alive in the nighttime—
A vampire of silence
drinking thoughts.
Easy, like a farmer eating lunch:
I'm consumed and consuming...
in love and being
loved, all at once.

How lovely, this inner peace.
I drink it all up while the world sleeps.

It comes alive in the nighttime
like a summer solstice fair.
It's a shining city beyond Olympus,
and all artists go there;
where it's always easy to find
untold universes
within this shining
city of the mind.

It can never be undone.
It comes alive with
the rising of the sun.

It's all a strange guidance,
how the creative mind provides
a natural alignment
we pull from somewhere divine:
A place without a name
or a location set in time.

Sunflower

It's hard to forget you
and all the lies that you've told.
Have I told you lately?
That I hate you?
I don't think so, no,
because I'm not sure that I do.

But I'm surely on the verge.
So, I'll send this deep breath in
to cleanse my words.
Let's start afresh please.
Deep breath again?
Oh yes, please.

See how you make me?
Isn't this crazy?
and whoever said
I wanted to be in love!
I'm not sure anymore.
This was all a doomed allure

filled with intrigue…
and now it's all gone it seems.

So, I run back to the sun,
the illuminated flower
that I have become.
And I ask for another—
a true lover and friend,
to share these days
until they come to an end.

But the sun was only
filled with a laughter,
so cold, it made me shiver.
He said, 'Child, if you're
looking for love,
go outside and look in a mirror.'

Selfish

Selfishly,
I'll keep me.
It's not so bad.
Don't worry,
I'll be fine…
In fact, I'm the best
I've ever had.

Now be on your way,
why don't you?
But before you do,

watch me wash away
the residue of you.
It's easy,
believe me,
you'll see how selfishly
I'll keep me away from you.

You will see me no more.

But rest assure of your blessings.
There are so many more
endless fishes in the sea,
with beautiful, precious colors,
that will all keep you company...
as you watch me not be blue,
as I selfishly keep
me away from you.

Booklover

If you have become lost to the world,
don't be afraid my sweet darling dear.
A power exists in books
but you must be there,

where,
you'll learn how life is
born from words,
as you escape into
this written universe.
A life without them
is a true curse.
Going half way
is just as worst.

There are so many worlds
within the world.
Books are treasures—
give them to little boys and girls.
What a pleasure

to have found you within youth.
I truly wouldn't
be the same without you.

It's a lovely thing to adore.
If you've become lost to the world,
go there;
you might find something
you've always been
searching for.

When Reality Shakes Up the Fairytale

There's a cobblestoned gardened path,
where the flowers and weeds
both feel the wrath of the wind.
She is here,
in a beautiful, yet, hurtful night.
She watches as angels lose
not only their wings,
but also their sight.

She knows it's all given for a price,
but still she drinks the wine of the dance.
And why couldn't she be more gingerly
in this terribly irresistible romance.

Now, near the cobble stoned
gardened pathway
paved with perfection,
she no longer drinks.

Half asleep under the leaves,
dazed with reflection,
she thinks:

What do you do
when your three wishes are spent?
And you're wondering of the sobering
and where everything all went?

The mustard seed is small,
but without it,
what is the final cost?
Do you fall?
Or do you rise
above what you've lost?

The Poets

They seem to lead
serenely tragic lives,
within a forevermore of fall,
because such beauty can only be born
from inner turmoil.

In the spring
they give voice to a beautiful pain.
Losing themselves
to where immortality is gained.

Lovely, they are.
They find a need to escape,
so, they crave spirits and space,
each one a star.

Within this Brotherhood of Man
the Creative Fire is open to all,
but few understand
that its purchase price
is the currency of life...

Of solitude and
contemplating…
Of a longing
unfathomable
to the uninitiated.

They can create hope
out of the hopeless.
Lovely they are:
The Poets.

Throw No Stones

Don't let them see you weak.
You must always stand tall,
and remember to think twice
before you speak or
none at all.
Fall if you must,
but get a grip and keep it going.
Cry if you must.
Everyone does,
even if they don't show it.

Just be who you are
in all your greatness and flaws.
The whole world
is but a stage after all.

And who are they
to judge anyone with
their laughter
or scorn them?
No one is perfect,

even Lucifer, the loser,
was once light of the morning.
And where is he now?
In nightmares and in movies?
In the shadows
of dark secrets
keeping things gloomy?

Or maybe he's still there at dawn.
Humbled now,
by how Angels fall,
and humbled now
at how God
forgives them all.

Among The Sons of Man

Sweet Prince of these
eternal dreams,
how can you ever understand
being in love with a phantom?

I feel like a mermaid
stuck on land,
but happily so,
hopeful to know
that he might be
among the sons of man.

It is the greatest need in me.
All darkness becomes undone,
for he is made completely
with ten trillion sparks from the sun.

A phantom built
by thoughts of love.

It bypasses all notions of reality.
It's a surety that a love
like this is some ancient sorcery.
You sing a sad love song
as I begin to understand,
that you've grown old
among the sons of man.

Sweet prince of these
eternal dreams,
now I see
that Love, sweet Love,
the mystery,
the legend,
is just a timeless love song
you sing from heaven.

Rome

Just the word alone is adored somehow.
It spells more all around
and calls for excesses that are easily found.
Its virtue is its vice.
And while its vices are
too nice for the common man,
all men are slaves to its hand.

The city for politics.
The country for those who pick
from nature's bounty.
Freedom, mysticism,
slavery, wisdom.
All in a melting pot
where nothing is hidden.

New roads.
Senators well composed.
Champions who live like kings.
Debauchery, mixed in
with the gnosis of things.

And all along with
the breeze and tragedies,
freeborn thinkers
try to understand,
not just the pretty things
but also, the will
and the ills of man.
They have stolen wisdom
and kidnapped Gods…
But what is to be will be.
Never in history
has there been a magic wand—
Just the Midas touch,
the undiscovered books,
and the magical breath—
so fragile that it's kept
hidden, deep in the atoms
where no one looks.

We Are What We Are....All Fallen Stars

For both the sinful
and the blessed lot,
to The Creator,
all of his Creations
must go back.

How easily they forgot…
all fallen stars,
walking around
within a heart that
knows itself not.
This must have been my wish.
I'm different.
I was born different
and I thoroughly enjoy this.

I wouldn't trade my place for yours
or take your hand design.
I too much love

the business of exploring this
God-given mind.
It is made from an
energy that is endless,
and with God's given time
I will use it until it's senseless.

I will not kneel.
I will not run around your tracks.
I'll find my own way
straight through your field...
imagine me...I know nothing...
but I know that.
There's no love that's owed to me.
I've found a skill
transforming ills
into poetry.

That's enough for one life.

I love this skin.
I love what shines within—
created by the brightest of lights.
And this, too,
is enough for one life.

It's remarkable
how energy never dies.
We are what we are...all fallen stars,
living only to rise.

Into the Forevermore of Dreams

It's just a silly childish dream
to be in love like this.
It's all a mist.
A vapor,
disappearing into
the forevermore of dreams.

This world is too cold for it,
it seems.
And it will tell you to
enjoy the romance
and dance while you still can.
Get the riches here
and buy peace for all your fears.
Young man,
the pain you give her
will make her stronger.
And you'll be given this gift

for just a little while longer.
So, what does she learn
that you don't?

That it is all just a mist.
A vapor,
disappearing into the
forevermore of dreams.

Little Dove

I fly high above their hate
to find a love and wisdom
that I can celebrate.
And even though some
part of this hurts my feelings,
another part makes me so strong
that it all makes no difference.
In fact, I might need this
more than I thought,
since I was born with an
Alchemist's heart.

Sadness is meant to be transmuted.
When in Zen, this is true
with nature and is no formality.
Whether as a sweet
melody or heavy metal,
I'm a rebel against
basic normality.

And the transformation occurs.
The butterfly flies
as hate gets transformed
into strengthening words.

It makes no difference
in the end.
It's all a blessing
to be taught the lesson
of knowing the foe
before we become friends.

How easily sweet it is,
to transform their hate into self love.

Yes, it's the sweetest thing.
And this is how you fly,
little dove.

Fear

What do we do with our dead
when they depart?
We bury the bones and keep the
memories in our hearts.
Life is a mystery we were
born to play.
Sometimes it's both
hard and easy.

What would Grandfather say?

Sadly, for me,
he died today.
But I've heard that
death isn't as we think it.
In a dream, he was an
ancient bird that paid me a visit.

And I hear his voice
as he sweetly sings,
that 'the world is the world,
let the inside of you
be forever spring.'

He said, 'live, grow,
know yourself
and understand,
you should read plenty and look up
as much as you can.

Learn your lessons
and find what you love,
because the fear of death
is not for when it comes...

But for a life not lived
and for dreams un-done.'

Cruise Control

Early this morning
there came a message from above,
that said be prepared to hurt
when you fall in love.

The faster you drive
the harder you crash.

Use cruise control
while coasting slower
than you have in the past.

Anything else
and your new love might not last,
and will just be
a sinking ship.

But who am I?
Still just a dreamer.
A believer,

and a reflection
of the thoughts that I think...

like how we should go
slowly sometimes
to watch it all grow.
No more driving fast
down roads we don't know.

A Prayer for All

For supreme guidance
and understanding,
in all our dealings, we pray.
In this way,
there will be true meaning
in each day.

Pray we know how
to sire our words.
I've heard, that if you
pray for patience
you'll be given chaos
in order to create
what you prefer.

All is in *Prana*.
All is free.
Always say your praises,
blessings come silently.

Pray for enlightenment
and mercy,
because life happens all the time.
Enlightenment... to pick apart
The Wise Men from
The Judas and The Clowns...
and mercy, so that none
of the nonsense
gets you down.

Jaded, yet Faithful

"No one loves me except my skin."
"This is all very woe—is—me—ish,
don't you think?"
"Yes, it is, I suppose;
and so it goes
in the sad times we're given—
it's all a wretched design."
"But despair is forbidden.
They say it's a sin
against the Holy Spirit's life."

"I've been so unwise, but Epiphany
has just given me eyes."
"Oh, is this a love song you want to tell?
Let me sit; it's all a dizzy,
spinning feel that knows no end.
You want to be in love,
but it's best to be in Zen.
Love is just a dizzy spinning feel.
It dies, only to begin again."
"Forgive me then,

as I was sipping too
deeply of love's sweet wine.
It took me so high,
then it took me so low,"
"Such is life my dear,
we do these things in order to grow."
"And what did I gain after all this time?"
"Only knowledge, which is the most sublime.
Only knowledge which can never be stolen
when in the midst of that beautiful mind.
What else on Earth did you think you'd find? Love?"
"Yes, of course, love,"
"You're more likely to find hate,"
"I'm not looking for that,"
"Doesn't mean it's not there to play."
"Love is the most desirable,"
"Yea, but it isn't reliable.
Love is fickle, you'll find.
Always influenced by the allure
of what is and what was left behind.

Love is knowledge, you'll realize,
when you finally get old.
It's in abundance for the mystics,
for the sages and for the bold.
It's the inner sun that can never go out.
It's the silent thing inside so few know about.
You are young, you know nothing."
"Yea, but it's the love of some God
that keeps the sun pumping.
You're bluffing, for this, I'm sad."
"Love *is* the bluff, it can drive you mad.
Knowledge, on the other hand,
is a must have.
Find knowledge first

and then you'll find the glory
because down here,
love is just a story.
It's the oldest story.
It's the coldest story."
"But it makes everything feel so warm,
and filled with betterment."
"You're a child, you know nothing."
"Just that love is heaven sent."
"Love is a sentiment.
It's just a drug that
stimulates the senses,
and then when it's gone
one becomes helpless.
We're all addicted to this joke…
to this myth.
Down here, even Divine Ones
can become jaded pessimists."
"I feel it too,"
"We all do…of love, the silly, cold, little coward."
"No…of love, the warm, the wise, divine power."
"Oh yes…Love, the wise.
It leaves you with the kind
of knowledge only it can provide.

What else on Earth did
you think you'd find?

Bliss

Everybody's
full of shit.
Literally!
Make
no mistake
and be not
surprised.

Sad to think…
We have all arrived
at this conclusion from
experience.

And while the love of
knowledge is a gift,
I sit here wishing I
could be one
with bliss…
in a childlike
innocence,
completely

ignorant
of all this.

Because everyone was
born filled with love,
make no mistake.
If only the world around us
wasn't so filled with hate.

Yes, the love of
knowledge is a gift.
And so is the childlike
ignorance of bliss.

Self of Steel

For all the bull dogs
who ever tried to bully me,
look at how I'm still
shining wonderfully.
A self of steel isn't
forged with cotton candy
or lollipops.
Only tougher things
that'll make a
weak heart politely drop.
This self of steel
is the true me,
it must be.
Shining wonderfully
and never rusty.
This self of steel
knows it's duty
as it shines
under this
skin and beauty.

From their swords
I don't need a shield.
I won't fight the feel
as steel sharpens steel.

Shining wonderfully
and never rusty.
There's a purpose for it all,
there must be.
A self of steel
won't ever complain
because there's
true power in pain—
trust me…
We just extract it.
No struggle is ever in vain.
In fact, it's an exact fit
for a self of steel.

The Good Life

When life comes in
and treats you
less than it should,
find pleasure
in understanding
that which needs to
be understood.
Find the best tunnel vision
under the sun.
Find the good life:
working smart,
making money
and having fun.
After that, the only
thing left to be done
is the assimilation of
these life lessons.

Knowledge and
understanding
is a blessing;
it's best to receive
them while we're young.
With them,
we can always make
a new life for ourselves,
as they come
with a blank canvas
and a paint brush.
Knowledge
and understanding:
without them,
we truly have
nothing much.

The Prince and Poor Man's Daughter

Particles of withered
hopes are discarded.
And now I'm lost within a dream
from which there is no release
or waters uncharted.
Why do you love me so deep?
Why will I ever want to retreat
from the invisible treasures
we dare to speak
or from the heights of love
we dare to reach.

You build me up, up out of my skin,
and so we live on pure air,
where angels dream, dance and sing
about the truest love
ever brought out from within.
This is O' so sweet:
A prince and a pauper.

You, the son of a king, and I,
a poor man's daughter.

How have we've found this true love song?
How do we live in two different worlds,
yet, come together as one?
Along with bliss we go.
Let me be loved by you
and you alone.
And now, it is so,
that your arms and your bones
have become my new home.

My hope floats
and my dreams come to life.
How can we go on
with this exciting delight?
This must just be a passing thing.
This is already the sweetest
love story with two authors,
who never knew they were
writing to begin with.

And if it ever becomes sad
I'll be happy to have had you
in my heart and in my hands.
Until then, he is here
at the dawn of summer's love,
with his sweet kisses that taste
like manna sent from above.
(If I'd ever tasted such a thing)

And as our cup over ran,
we flew together on the
edge of a dove's wing.
Below, there were the Fates,
and Pan,
(who forgot to drink
from the cup in his hand)
with all the others who
listened as the Muses
sang towards the heavens...

that he is mines,
and I am his,
most treasured friend,
that is pleasured and
fed by his very presence.

With such sweet serenity,
I have become the best of me.
We cling together
like the shore to the sea.
I call to him
like how the flower
calls the bee.

My sweet Prince.
He gives his security,
and I give my honor.
Gladly we share
because what else
do we have to offer?
And when he leaves,
nothing is as sweet as
dreaming of tomorrow.

Because he always returns,
to find me along the banks,
day-dreaming and
loving myself
as Narcissus once had.
And like the lake,
I see myself in his eyes.
Then together we earn
the prize for our sacrifice.

How fun is this love!
We run to where
two become one.
We enjoy the myths
and the mysteries.
Free days of pondering are spent
on Herodotus's *Histories*...
on *Ovid* and, of course,
Solomon's Songs we did not neglect.
Oh, the spark of intelligence!
It carries us to find
Nature's evidence of all truths.
In this celestial youth
our spirits understand that
the vehicle of the flesh
is but a chariot for the stellar man,
as he sits upon the throne of the mind;
with its unseen wings,
able to fly away at any time.

And so, we fly.

Disappearing into ourselves,
finding the Divine.

The To Do List

Keep looking within.
There, lingers all that we seek:
Alignment.
Refinement.
Love…
all within reach.

Save more money.
Say more things laced with honey.
Play and smile some more.
Get frowns to be upside
down some more.
Create Zen.
Give poetry to the hearts of Men.
Appreciate each and every day.
Constantly grow.
Constantly give praise.

This Day

This day is your own
and not mines.
The memory is there
only for you to find.
Oblivious to me,
suddenly, I'm here.
But way before this
you felt me everywhere.

Even though today's my birthday,
I'm thinking of you,
and not me,
because without you
where would *I* be?

And even though
life wasn't always easy, no,
I must tell you
that I appreciate you
for all that you went through,

on this day,
all those years ago.

For keeping me safe and warm.
For receiving a bothersome stranger
into loving arms.
My first best friend.
My very first love.
You do your best
and that's what you've become.

I love you better
than what these words can say.
How amazing you are,
for what you did on this day.

Nosy Nostalgia

Life is such a trip.
Of it we'll spend a fraction
lamenting opportunities missed
and chances unseized…
given over to inaction.

The Queen that I am,
I met a handsome King one day.
He gave me some wildflowers
then went on his way.
Freely, peacefully,
eyes met.
Paths crossed so easily,
it was a hook up from
God himself.
It all happened so naturally,
and he was actually
the perfect match for me.

But life is funny
when you're 'too busy'.
And I was dreaming
my life away so much,
that I didn't see when to life
my dreams came
straight to me, in a rush…
with stargazers,
with tulips,
with wildflowers.
And why didn't I shower
you with kisses?
Why? When your presence
felt so delicious?

Nosy nostalgia,
As it seems, my feelings
don't matter.
But I'm a trooper so,
I'll soon recoup…
from missing
my lost love…
all I need is wildflowers
and soup.

We should just explore love,
but yea,
life and love
is funny that way:
How magic
happens for us
while we look
the other way.

Fully Bloomed

If they hate you now
when you're the regular you,
what will they do
when you've fully bloomed?
Let them go crazy
within that hateful, living hell,
because maybe,
just maybe, they
might one day kill that old self…

And leave no letter,
while transforming themselves
into something better,
And find comfort in the
arms of Wisdom,
where she'll tell her
immature children,
that when you hate
others due to envy felt deeply,

you're really hating you...
Only the You, you wish
you could be.

So, Bright Lights,
we keep a flashlight
to analyze these rooms.
Bright Lights keep a flashlight,
so bright, that it gives them gloom.
Because if they hate you now,
when you're the regular you,
what will they do when
you've fully bloomed?

Refined

We are all beautiful,
but some of us
are more refined.
Some of us
don't know we're diamonds,
while others are satisfied
being a dime.

Beauty is in the eye
of the beholder,
but what if the beholder
isn't wise?
Beauty is thus
a beautiful
lie.

Of All Times and Places

This paper here
is riddled with teardrops,
but fear not
for the sight of them...
for there's light inside
of them aplenty.
And the lesson
I've learned, if any,
is that living is amazing
and a bit dangerous too.
But we are conquerors
of adversity—
this is what we were born to do.

So amazing and crazy,
this life given to me.
Sadness mixed with happy,
comedy meets tragedy.

A song for this amazing
and crazy life given to me.
Where else in the universe
would I dare to be?

Making Light

The way you make me feel is a trap.
It's all a masquerade
that needs to fade to the back
and then fade
forever more into black.

I have no fear
so, put me there.
Let me be a light
in the darkness of space.
A light in the darkness
of my mother's womb,
where it was warm and safe.

Yes, it's a trap.
So let it fade to the back,
and then fade forevermore
into black...

Into Dark Matter.
In the end, we're all left alone
to climb Jacob's Ladder.

This knowledge is a savage.
How does it all vanish
when learning is my will?
I must take the mess of this
and make light of it still.

Missed Kisses

What kind of love is this
and within what world?
Oh, it's a comedy,
where he laughs at the girl.

You make me wonder
why I was ever even born.
What kind of a love is this?
There are no roses,
only thorns.

I had on blinders.
Wisdom was lost to me
and I had to find her.
I'm universal,
but he makes me feel so small.
I'm afraid I'll run into your kind again,
so I walk this path analyzing all.

I'm not going crazy about it.
I'm doing just fine without it.
This topic has grown tedious.
There's nothing more you have
that I am in need of.

For all the wisdom gained,
this is a fair trade.
Now, blinders, go find your maker.
Come, amnesia
to make him a stranger.

A broken heart
calls for strange wishes.
But all it ever
wanted
were your kisses.

Life for the Living

Lost in confused mazes...
These phases that he grows through
keeps his thinking process on ten,
times two.

His state of mind is always
planning for those
'what ifs',
As he is in his own pit
of loneliness...
wanting and waiting
to be uplifted
from the solitude
in which he dwells alone.

It stretches past everything
down to the depths of his
personal hell,
which is that of being broke.

And he's thought of selling his soul,
but fears he might now be too old.
So, he borrows time like words to melodies,
soaring high to where it's heavenly
and not so cold.

But as
Gravity calls all back,
he goes on
with the business
of growing stacks.

Making his life livable.
Changing the rigged game,
making it winnable.

Champions

How far we've come
with the things we've seen
and the understanding we've cultivated!
Though under-rated,
look how high we fly
with damaged wings.
How wonderful that
Champions can emerge
from broken things!

We can never doubt ourselves
for we know not
why we were created.
Whatever greatness that may
lay ahead of us
is yet to be seen.
In the meantime
we'll keep our eyes open
and gravitate towards
our living dreams.

And if something comes
to set you apart from yourself,
never stay away too long.
The world needs you
my love.
Who else can
sing your songs?

Loving

Love songs sings true
of the sweetest thing on planet blue.

Like Rumi, Hafiz, McKay and Hughes,
only the Lovers truly know of you...
and they know this too:
of how love exists within
and cannot be subdued;
not even by the laws of men
or even by the chainsaws of men.
Not even by you,
the strongest of them.

My love,
we are only here because of it.
And the young, we
bear the effects from all of it...
Blindly. Silently. Wisely.

Love: even the thought of it
is a blessing.
Whatever the cause of it,
we should be thankful.

Human Nature

Knowledge is a power
that is unending.
Be a student of something
or have your mind
be devoured by
something less friendly.

Be a student of something—
whatever you like,
until you master the game
and can teach others to fly.

Be a student of something—
there's so many to choose.
Try your sweet luck,
you probably won't lose.

Be what you love
and enter into favor.
Be what is in line
with your center

and your creator.
Be what you must,
create your own flavor.
But most of all,
be a student of Human Nature.

Here no one
gets to choose.
Not even the monks.
Not even the fools.

From birth,
until one becomes one
with the Earth
or funeral fire,
humans will always surround him
whether or not this is his desire.

From the first step
until the last regret,
they are there whether as foe or kin.
Why not understand them,
the pleasantries and
dangers that lie within?

We often walk the fine line
between brilliance and insanity.
But to understand
the quirks and anomalies
of the human mind...
while some require
years of study,
others need only
a moment in time.

Silly Rabbit

Superman?
What a fib.
You look like him
but you don't
act like him.

Superman?
Man, you wish you were him.
But, yes, this love was
built on lies.

This was a prank
when I was blind,
but now
I give thanks for
opened eyes.

Just look at him go.
He lingers on the surface
because he doesn't think
a deep thought.

Just look at him go.
He'll forever be
hopping…
there's no stopping
the game of hearts.

The Un-dying

We're all the same.
In the invisible world
we find bliss
as we contemplate.

We live to create.
The doing so of which
is usually built on great pain

And those Master Poets,
they don't even have to rhyme.
What takes me a song,
they convey
in one line.

They are legends on a pedestal.
I'm just a girl
playing with words
at their feet.
But I was born old

within a new world
and so, we meet.

It's the creative fire
that they all used.
Shakespeare, Goethe
and Voltaire too.

It's the spark
that started it all.
Giving power
to creative creatures
both large and small.

We all linger there,
within the lovely affliction—
An invisible addiction:
creating life out of pure air.

There's a grapevine
between artists
and the Divine.
Inspiration finds them,
even when they try to hide.

It's the spark
within the dark
that called to them,
because they were in tuned:

Morrison, Rice, Picasso
Hess and Hughes.
Da' Vinci, Bukowski, Poe
and all the best of them.
(And even those we never knew.)

The Greats,
my friends,
will always be alive.
Look for them.
They live within
their creative designs.

You Love Me

All things are possible
with you, of course.
My thoughts are yours,
my heart is yours.
My life is yours.
Please help me to use them wisely
for the proper cause.

My intimate relation with you
is what matters much.
Even if everything
shatters and falls to dust.

My spirit adores you,
and my flesh applauds
you for your greatness.
Knowledge of you is sacred.
If I chase anything,
I will chase it
and all else will come together.
You've given me the perfect measure

of all things:
Beauty, pleasure, grace—
even of pain.
The result is all the understanding
I have and will gain.

Let me go on and on forever
about how much life is clever.
You are in all the elements.
You sculpted the essence of beauty
in all its elegance.
You are in every nucleus.
You are the most sublime.
Even in the womb,
it was you with us,
writing your designs.

You are the string that binds.
You are the sun that shines.
You are the mind that forms the planets,
sets them on their orbits,
then creates magic when they align.
A mathematician,
an architect,
a believer.
A scientist,
an artist,
a dreamer.
A queen or a king.
The writer
and co-signer of all things.
The invisible force is the real Boss.
Love, Nature, Gravity, Clarity—
the maker of man
and all that he sees.

I feel lovely.
Why should I ever be afraid?
Even before I was born,
you loved me
and knew my name.

Whoever You Are

I don't know it all about God
and neither do you, little dove.
But whoever made this earth,
her sun and moon,
I love.

My life is yours.
My heart is yours.
How majestic,
these planets
and all else that you've built.
You've given me this life to live,
and at the end of it,
whether luxurious or small,
I will tell you what I've done—
offenses and kindnesses, all.

I was told to never lean
on my own understanding,
so, I stand tall with an opened mind.
I find that curiosity is my guilt.

To that I'll humbly admit
as I sit here nested within
this temple that you've built.

Let me spend the rest of
this time making you proud.
None of it matters—
what they think quietly or say out loud.
Inside I'm still just
a child amazed at how
the sun and moon
follows me around.

I'm amazed at how nature
tastes and smells so sweet.
Amazed at how she is you
and he is she.
You are the power behind
all these stars.
Bless you,
God, Goddess, Allah.
Hidden Beloved One,
Father Ptah.
I love you.
I thank you,
whoever you are.
Take this song of love.
May it bring joy to you.
I love you in all the names
that we may call to you:

God, Goddess, Allah.
Beloved son Heru.
Universe, Nature, Creator.
Jesus, the Guru.

The Oneness of Man

Since every heart
comes with its own
baggage,
you want to
sort of
take away from the load
and not add to it.

Smiles,
hugs,
kisses and jokes…
Sweet nothings filled
with love and hope
can make it all better.

So, here's a kiss
wrapped in a letter,
with a hug and a smile,
with the hope to lighten
the load for a while.

There's no formula,
no secret for living.
You can only do the best
with what you've been given.

I'll bring honey
each time we meet.
We're all the same.
A good life
and love we seek.

The world is the world.
It seems it'll never end…
And since we're all here together,
then we might as well be friends.

The Lonely Side of Town

You left me here in my lonely bed,
with my lonely self,
and my lonely frown,
in the loneliest room
of my lonely home,
on the loneliest side
of my lonely town.

This is where all the pretty girls,
with broken hearts,
make not a retort of aloe-vera bitterness.
Instead, they eat it and forgive
and then shake it off
because why be blue, singing sad songs,
when you can be a happy shade of golden bronze?
They'll dry their eyes
and then moisturize,
because, even as the pillows cry with truth,
you have no choice but to be brave
and find a lesson inside you.
Or else all this pain will be in vain.

The hopes of what is true
is that the emptiness will end
and they will begin anew;
That the broken pieces will
mend themselves with time,
or by some strange invisible glue.

And soon the tears disappear
and the fears calm down,
because as steel strengthens steel,
beauty and love will always be around.
I guess that's why you're here,
hugging me now
and loving me now.
Yes, I'm aware of how
the sun still shines
even here,
on the lonely side of town.

Love Drunk

You don't love me
the way you should,
and this makes
me miserable.
I hate that I love you.
I hate that you're so
irresistible.

We started building,
and then you disappeared.
What kind of a house is this?
I'm the only one here.

You shouldn't be so sexy.
You shouldn't be anywhere
but home,
right next to me.
He's a bad boy,
but I enjoy him.

He knows all the pretty girls
want to employ him,
so it's easy to be himself...
just like a king.

You punk.
I'm love drunk
and always have been.
Yes, it's the feeling.
He's sweet, so he lets me have it.
But how is a girl going
to beat this bad habit?
He's in my bones.
He's in my dreams.
I find aspects of him
in all that I see.

I love you too much
I suppose.
We're love drunk,
but we find our way home.

The Con of Men

Let's sing a song for the con of men.
To the con of men let's sing an ode.
My, oh my, how loud the crickets are,
with no one there at the show...
for we all know of the con of men.

They arm their harm then
wash the wrongs from them.
They tell lie after lie,
writing sincere songs on them.
They paint gray
metallic flowers pretty,
saying 'they're beautiful, aren't they?'
They create the hell
in which we live in...
speaking of heaven,
but showing us the wrong way.

The world of men can be sad.
What will save
us from this place?
Put transcendence in your plans…
The kind you cannot buy
and you cannot take.

For the life of me
I try to comprehend
not just the pretty things,
but also the con of men.

But, because life and
death roll hand in hand,
it'll take a thousand
years to understand.
So let us all sing the ode,
and continue to pretend
that we just don't know.

Stardust

"A smudge and
a half goes very far.
What are you so afraid of—?
you already know life can be hard."

"Indeed! It is harder
than I thought.
It seems that the will to live
and the death wish
comes together
in the same heart."

"But it's all just a school,
with stages and rules
and sages and fools."

"Yes, and we're all afraid
while waiting for
God to help us,"
"It comes from within…"
"And you with your halo and wings!

What do you have in common
with us lowly things?"

"Only transcendence and will...
But still little dove,
it's all just a school
with stages and rules,
and sages and fools
who must all be
as brave as love.
If you look to the stars,
they'll tell you that
you are a reflection
of the same stuff
they're made of.

One day you'll see
the light in yourself:
a celestial being
trapped in a canopy of flesh.
Born only to learn,
here in this school
with its stages and rules.
Becoming sages from fools.

"It's hard,"
"For now, but then it gets easy.
Everything you need is here,
you just cannot see it.

We all must be
as brave as love.
Get it together, you must!
You magnificent
little speck of stardust."

Lioness

Because being weak will never do.
Because what's the point in loving,
if you can't love through and through?

Because lust is too easy.
Because deceit is cheesy.
Because of being a lioness
with an armor of golden steel,
I've found my ultimate bliss
at the top of this wheel.

I see it so clearly,
that it's not so dear to me.
It's all a dizzy feel.
When I was a cub it was fun
now I only love

looking at the horizon,
and bathing in the sun.
Knowing full well
that we are one
and one alone.

This trip is just a test
set in faraway land...
passing only if I find
my way home:

Back to myself.
Back to my eternal spirit
encased within this flesh.

This is where I get my glow.
This is where I receive all blessings,
both known and unknown.

This is from where
understanding comes.
In times of sadness
this is where I run to.

It is there
that the complex
becomes simple.

She's a lioness.
She stands apart.
She counts her wealth by the stars.

This lioness,
golden and majestic,
is reflecting
atop this wondrous wheel.

It keeps going around and round.
Where is the real appeal?

Yes,
bathing in the sun.
Knowing full well
that we are one.

True Love

You treat her badly,
but that's okay.
God treats her like
the princess that she is—
and you'll see someday,
no matter how far,
that you're not as wise
as you think you are.

He gives us true love—
There can be none better.
He changes sad love songs
into Athenian letters.
And we save them
for all the fools in love,
and that are blind,
about a true love
not here on earth to find.

Not because it isn't there,
but because we were already

born with this love that knows no end.
How sad, we spend our time trying to
find it outside of ourselves.

It is there.
It blooms when it needs to...
Easily attracting its equal.

So, let's love ourselves
truly and magnificently,
so that our truest love
may come to be.

Intuition Told Me

Intuition told me,
but it was I
that turned a deaf ear.
Now after all my troubles,
I am back here.
A bit ashamed,
I must say,
until I heard intuition brag
of how tomorrow is another day,
with gifts to have
and no time to give away to
unnecessary sadness.

To be afraid of this
mysterious life we are living
makes no sense.
I conclude
that I will dive
into the eternal youth.

But easy does it.
Intuition said nothing of this.
At first,
it came as a burst of clarity.
I was about to fail myself
and intuition said that
I'd have to perform self charity.
You cannot run and hide.
Life is how you make it.
Let us all make it an endless
cherry pie or
sweet potato custard.

But easy does it.
Intuition comes before
all that ever is or ever wasn't.
Intuition is wise.
Listen well
and you'll never be surprised.

So Sure

I am so lost without you.
My bubble of happiness has
been busted and torn.
This is no longer a gift, but a curse,
because I've been so immersed
in you, who I've trusted,
and now you're gone.

You have abandoned me
and I should abandon you.
But it's not so easy when
everyone looks like you.

You're a crook.
Yes, you who have stolen my heart.
You're such a jerk and
I must tell you that this is
no longer going to work.

I will get over you, before long.
In the end, it will be like it was before...
When I was strong.
When the lady in the
mirror was so sure.

Wisdom of the End

Get over the past.
There's no use for this path.
Wrath goes undone.
Clouds flee
with the rising
of the sun.

Beautiful flower growing,
going along with the wind.
Who else understands you
better than your skin?

What are mistakes
but steps you mistook?
We must use them to prevail.
Life has informational books
like what
the sages have said
of the so many things we overlook,
and still all is well.

So now I'm done
with the foolish path.
My wrath is now Zen.
I will go back to the beginning
with the wisdom of the end.

Sunrise

We live to become wise
do we not?
In the dark,
we now see truth
while everyone lies a lot.

Love is the sunrise.
It makes cold hearts melt.
It eases storms
when a pure
single ray is felt.

I fly high
to where he lives
and down below
I see that they all need love.
Misery and sorrow only lives
because of the lack thereof.

And so, we grow
and have come to know
that in a world of opposition,
the brave will never fold;
happy to be like
the sunrise,
with an inner light
that never grows old.

The Birth of Reason

A little dove filled with
not for nothing smiles.
She lives less on the ground
and more in the sky.
She's just a child and
there's a thing that she does:
playing with her hair in the mirror,
messing with Mommy's make-up.

Then out of nowhere
she feels a feeling that
created a thought:
that for the first time she
listened
well to the beat of her heart.
Her eyes felt more open,
and the air, too, felt strange.
So, she stopped what
she was doing and
decided to pray.

It was going well:
'Our Father who art in heaven...'
(I'm sure we all know our prayers well,
or at least knew them better
when we were seven.)
It was going so well
she almost fell to rest,
until she felt herself
inside herself;
hiding inside the
beating part of her chest.

There, she was sure that
she wasn't alone.
There was a voice,
ancient and wise,
very much not her own.

"Who are you child?"
"Who are you?"
"I am the Holy Spirit
within your mind.
You don't know me yet,
but I'm here for you to find.

I am a gift from the Gifter.
If He is Father,
then I am Mother.
Life can be your tester
and at times your oppressor,
but we will be your up-lifters."

And they talked for a while.
Holy Spirit listened well
to secret questions and thoughts
that she couldn't ask
and couldn't tell.

Then Holy Spirit said:
"You'll seek truth and love...
and for all your days,
with a light heart,
you'll carry them.
She said:
"Holy Spirit, I'll let your will
be my will,
though I can't
make any promises."

Or so it seemed.
The child remembered
the adventure years later
when it all
became a dream.
But somehow
it had to be true.
The voice remained
the same,
it was only the little girl
who grew.

Trading Comfort for Insight

It's cold tonight.
Winter laughs at this
Summertime sadness
as she falls,
and we all soon call
out to Sister Spring
to rescue us from him.

Winter is a fright.
Even the stones know
of how he tends to hold,
shaking you down to your bones,
shattering the warm
myths that you like.

I'll be rewarded
for my efforts in time.
How kind,
insight eventually
brings peace of mind.

This cold
is a strange bedfellow,
wise and true.
In the spring, we'll retire
like new part-time lovers do.

For all the sad things
that might happen,
insight rise
with their passing.

Yes, it's cold tonight.
But I'm perfectly fine,
up, trading sweet comfort
for wonderful insight.

Sun and Moon

You've traveled with me all along,
listening without judgment,
as I sing my songs.
I love them...these two.
They say only the lonely
talk to the sun or moon,
but I'd be lonely without your lights.

I love them.
These two,
they give freely without a price.
They witness all,
yet they'll never tell your secrets—
not for your whole life.

But for happiness, don't find it yet.
Whatever they overlook, Nemesis and
and Conscience won't forget.

I love them.
These two,
they are immortals after all.
They were here
before you were born,
and will be here
long after you're gone.

The Dance (In Zen)

The chemical romance
is all in the dance of life.
We cannot fail to understand it.
Our very existence demands it.
This dance of life where strife
can make you stronger than love,
and tons of money
can't buy nothing
but suds, drugs and woes...
and vampires who
look like friends
who you really don't know.

But wisdom comes in the end.
If not, then what is this all for?
Only awareness,
that lives on forevermore.
This dance of life

is a search for balance.
And who knew
it all started from one chalice!

Make no mistake...
Let it be clear:
you will always retake the test
until you finally pass
and learn to dance,
while showing no fear,
to the vipers that are
absolutely everywhere.

All things divide
and I understand why,
it's not all such a mystery
as I close my eyes.
Yes, it can be a blur,
but I see it all when deep in Zen.
It makes the dance easier.
I go back there,
again and again.

Dreams of a Daisy

Well here I am,
listening to leaves twirl.
Thinking of what to do
if I ruled the world.

It's a dream I dare
to dream sometimes.
It's a song I remember
but haven't heard for a while.

Thinking you'll have fun,
but it's always easier
thought than done.
It's a bit much, you'll find.
Yet we'll do it anyway
for all of mankind.

It's a silent power play and
a game of chess with the Creator.
It's the unseen hope for the days
of maybe being our own savior.

It's lovely,
but yea, it's a bit crazy.
Of ruling the mountain
are the dreams a daisy.

Bright Light

Your light shines bright and strong.
It's a reflection of the sun's glory…
Surely, some won't be
able to take it for long.
So, if you're friendless
don't be surprised.
But, really, who cares,
since a Sunny Valentine
will shine, all the while, unknowingly
attracting butterflies and red eyes
from everywhere.

You're a friend,
no doubt.
But Bright Light,
Bright Light, some of them
want you to go out.
Yes, Bright Light, Bright Light,
some of them hate us,

but, in some way, they all want a touch.
Maybe we shine too bright.
Maybe we shine too much.

You're a friend,
no doubt.
But Bright Light,
Bright Light, some of them
want you to go out—
down deep into their depths.
They so do love the dark,
what else did you expect?
Except, Bright Lights:
they only live for the bang.

And that's all the
God and Goddess sang...
to brighten up the dark.
To watch the vampires
and demons all shit
themselves apart.

Never Forget to Laugh

He lives in the Bible,
while I live in the sky.
Full of life and love
we were, for a moment,
until he sent me to the place
where thoughts go to die.

Sun-less diet.

Here I am, in the place
he sent me to find.
It's disturbing.
It's unworthy of any
of my time.

Sun-less diet.

Can't get my heart anymore broken,
so, I've vowed to be silent.
The twilight comforts me—
It is beautifully quiet.

But when shall it pass?
Only God knows.
In the meantime,
my task is continual growth.

The love of God,
Prana,
is all over Gaia,
and it is constantly hugging me.
But this sadness is bugging me,
and when shall it pass?
I swear, when this vow
of silence is over,
I'll never again forget to laugh.

De-toxing From Stupid Cupid

I dismiss you and your fairytales.
Real true love no longer exists—
you tricked me with your inventions.
Now I'm de-toxing with vodka
and ale for my pain.
My once plumped lips are now pale
because he stole all my kisses;
or was it I that gave them away in vain?

For too long closed down shut,
now these eyes have opened up.
I've been looking on the brighter
side of things.
I will eventually sober up,
then you will be the crying king.

My eyes open further
and I see that we are all in a merger.

Take your bow, you lousy pretender.
I am no longer afraid of this stage
or of the actors around me
and how well they play.

See, under our olden sunrise
nothing is really new,
like heartbreak lullabies
and tragedies of what is true.

Love has become a bore.
So I'm detoxing from
Stupid Cupid,
and feeling better
than I did before.

Re-discovery

Searching for a new love that is pure.
Tell me where can I find you?
Come with me, you will be adored,
as I will always be kind to you.

Oh, reciprocity, where did you go?
Did you take honesty with you
as you went down the road…
to have a drink
with the noble pimps
and all the gracious hoes?
Let's be honest—
what else is there to do?
Let's be honest—
who has time for sadness
or for being blue?

Sober from when
you held me in your charms.
It wasn't long ago

that you were my tutor,
but I had to forget
what you taught.

I was once searching for a new.
I found and now I understand you.
The realest love is
yet to be re-discovered.
It includes only me
and my books
underneath the covers.

My love, I'm a mystic.
My heart is a gem.
Poetry is my lipstick.
Love will free us all.
Then again, perfection flees us all
and leaves us all here.
We are but mortal men.

Who Lingers There?

You're much better than I,
though we've been
together my whole life.
You fly at the speed of light,
granting me valuable insight.

You are a learner
but who are you?
You are an observer
but who are you?
You're high off life
with just air and sunlight.

A flower
with divine power,
who sees
that all things must pass,
so, to waste not these hours,
we believe in

and is constantly empowered
by our dreams.

There you are all
content and serene.
Yes, all things must pass.
We fear the unseen
while you laugh
an eternal laugh
and sing,
that our spirits are immortal—
death is nothing to fear.
The problem is
all the wonderful things
we must leave here.
(But just for a little while,
since nothing with God's
energy can ever really die.)

It's only the senses
that conjure up fear.
Inside, a warrior lingers there
within the silence,
who needs nothing more
than universal guidance.

Who lingers there
within the peace?
When I'm upset,
you're at ease.
Who lingers there
within the light?

Who dares me to
dream for things
not within my sight?

If life has a
mirrored reflection
we cannot see, then
who lingers there?
Who else but me!

The Perfect Kingdom
Built by Love and Wisdom

An ode to he
who would be wise
with truth seeking:
live and dream completely
and utterly to the fullest
of your being.
The key to life is to
make the two become one lens.
Therefore, your beast and your angel
must become friends.

There is a Supreme Goddess that lives.
She's beautiful, invincible, and easily gives.
She searches for truth
and indulges in a knowledge so rear,
she meditated under her favorite tree
for a thousand years.

She's always inspired
and never tires.
She enjoys the comedies
and is always grateful to see
angels and demons both smile
at sad caterpillars transforming
into armored butterflies.

She has a home inside of herself,
made of peace, ease
and creative magnificence.
But still with a solitary heart to wish upon,
she became weary of her thoughts.
And one night, when the
moon was full and warm,
she slipped away into her lover's arms.
Now, he knows all things,
but his favorite time
is when she sings.
So, under a blur from the juice of the palms,
they wrote songs of truth.
Then for a thousand years
of sun and moon,
she played the bride
and he played the groom.
They have full joy
on days of heat
and nights of cool,
in their sacred room
ornate with jewels.

It's a love so easy and serene,
they linger together,
even in their dreams.
They create magic
when they make love.
The one below,
the other above.

It's a balance that
can never be out of sync.
What his winter destroys
she brings back in the spring.
It's an understanding that
doesn't need words to speak.
And every second is a day,
as they play on silk sheets.
But she awakes to a calling
as her sweet darling sleeps.
Finding her way back in
between two worlds of being;
sitting there with closed eyes,
yet all seeing.
He awakes to his lonesome
and takes her once more,
while the stars and
planets applaud them
for finding an ancient love
so rear and pure.

She is love
and he is wisdom.
Together they've built
the perfect kingdom.

Fame

Sometimes what we seek
is nothing neat,
but it is sought none the less.
The world is not always shiny,
and yes,
no lesson is learned untimely.
To deal with it wisely
is highly acclaimed,
and yet so few have found that fame.

But I know some of those few—
painted the same *Homo-sapien* hue.
They say the secret lives within,
and while that should be clear,
the world keeps us spinning,
and too busy to go there.

Yet, we must,
because the world is unjust
and grimy,
with no lesson
learned untimely.
To deal with it wisely
is highly acclaimed,
and that is
the ultimate fame.

Namaste Times Two

Namaste one:
The light in me
honors the light in you.

Namaste two:
The shadow in me
sees the shadow in you.

But light has more speed.
In fact, a little bit of light
is all you'll need.
So why be afraid?
In time, we'll understand
these two, as we should…
that we are all one
or two of the same.
If we are wise,
we will choose the good.

Venus, My Love

Venus, my love
on your sweet day,
my lips are yours...
there are lovely things to say

Let Love come play with us.
Hear me my love:
What's to life
if you're not here with us
and your absence is felt?
The birds will cease to sing
and the snows will never melt.

And yes,
while strength is necessary,
I'm just a young
sweet berry you see,
Venus, my love,
I love you every day.
If lost, we live for the quest to find you
so, please, let Love come out and play.

Hear me, my love:
give me the truest of you,
because Venus, my love
I love you,
I do.

Tragic Mathematics

How can I thank you?
My love will find the words and the ways.
The words will fill the page.
The page will be delivered,
but you will be too busy to hear its case.
And yet, I love you.

I just wanted you to know,
That I miss you when we fight…
That I cannot sleep without you…
I am so cold tonight.

Can we stop our little antics?
I know that love is patient
and I need this talent.
This is such tragic mathematics,
and I was never any good at it.

Have I failed?
I pray, you say 'no'.
Forgive me, my love,

I'm still learning as I go.
I run to Zen again.
Let me discontinue with this
saddened path.
Zen again.
Intriguing like when
we first met
and it was love at last.

Whence They Come

When the words stir
and create a song,
I dare to think
from where they come.

Is it really me?
What is this
Imaginative faculty?

I have sung praises for days
since I was a little girl,
abiding with the creative,
taking myself away
from this cold world.

I am native to this thought place.
Initiated long before
I received my first heartache.

Oh, to visit where the greatness dwells.
Here, all is well.
Living is just a tale to tell.
What a privilege it is to be here
and to know that it never ends.

Cinderella With a Gun

Cinderella has dried her
tears with the sun.
When her father died
she went on the run.
No more scared little girl,
she's now become Cinderella with a gun…
Cinderella who understands
the way of things—
both bitter and sweet.

No more scared little girl.
She has come to see
that when they're all unkind,
strength and courage
are the friends you'll find…
there, all along, on the inside.

So, she meditates for fun.
Finding peace easily,
so, if Charming comes
she'll know it for sure.

And maybe the world
will have more meaning then—
much more than it had before.

But for now
she doesn't need that part.
She's become
Cinderella with a gun...
Cinderella much more smart.

And now she's found
a place, under the royal sun,
to build her castle in silence.
Her invisible gun
filled with understanding
and kindness.

Brooklyn Summer Nights

The longings of my youth still shine bright.
Love and dreams are still aplenty
so, still, we feast on life.
Brooklyn summer nights...
What a blessing.
We were allowed
the errors of adolescence.

Now that I'm grown up
I easily still feel for it.
Feeling like I want to go back
to the Block or to Briton Beach,
on those nights we were free,
running away from
sorrows with comic relief.
Those were the olden times
that feel like yesterday...
where the stress of life didn't mess
with our smiles as we'd play.

Now we have bills calling.
Stay working out, to prevent the skin from falling.
Advancing, romancing.
Bringing little ones into the
fold of things.
Holding on to your queen or your king—
And the most important one
that lives within.

There are reasons
to appreciate the changing seasons
and all that comes with it.
As it seems, nothing is missing.
But like holidays filled with cake,
I'm always trying to get back to that place
where the wind filled my face with kisses...
before I had my first kiss.
Before I got my heart broken.
Before I understood fear.
I never knew I'd miss those days—
sometimes hoping for a token
to take me back there.

And we still go back with a few cups,
watching the moon, as she glistens over us.
No bon fires like within the sixties;
just thankful my friends are still with me.
And I realize how much I miss
these innocent thoughts of another time;
before anything in the world
tried to take a hold on our minds.
I'm withstanding a sadness
that I cannot find the words for.

All the while, I pray more
for the understanding that I seek.
A deep breath brings my relief,
so, I smile very sweetly.
Life and living can be so wonderful
as it passes very quickly.

Merci

All this drinking won't consume me.
It's all to the fun and good
but it won't ever rule me.
At this age
I must engage in this,
so that I won't ever say
that I've ever missed.

I was told to hit every wave,
so, every day I play like I'm Hawaiian:
forever tanning,
forever loving our one and only sun.
Already loving the Goddess
I will eventually become.

It is indeed the climb.
We can all be so much better

if we dared to try.
Let us all be all that we can we be.
Let me take my own advice
and get rid of these vices in me.

All this drinking is a mercy I'm told.
We fall when we're small,
but become wise before we're old.
This life is quick,
but the experience of this
is a surety of glory for the bold.

So...

All this drinking won't
consume us—
no, not yet.
But all thanks will
be given now
in case
we forget.

The Maze

Creativity creates
happiness every day—
That's what the mind's for,
so, to your own self
make your wish.

And let your heart
not be hardened by
these life lessons—
that's what wine's for,
so, let's all take a sip.

Get a grip
and hold it steady.
Life is such a trip,
better show them
babies how to be ready.

Life can be a doozy of a daze.
We are all a part of the club.

The journey is a maze
that can seem quite empty as we
all walk or run.
Some more faster than some.

We all fall,
but some don't ever get up.
They become stuck in this place,
living to die.
While others spend their days
at work or at play
trying to fly,
far away from this maze.

Power and Freedom

The roads to success are not always legal.
But when you're above it all,
with concentrated power,
laws are given to seagulls to devour.

Too wide the gap.
Too dark a map to follow.
The truth might be too hard to swallow,
but ignorance is no bliss—
It's the trap that leads to sorrow.
Oh, to remember the clues we were given.
There from the beginning,
now they are hidden.

Survival calls for strength
and not so much of honor.
The soldier needs less of chivalry
and much more of armor.
Don't worry about the genius—
he knows what he's doing.
Plus, negativity is an Alchemists' tool,

since they know what to do with it.
In other words,
let's all mind our own business
and of your own self
never become bored…

Potentiality is always stored.
It's the flesh that
produces its own hindrance
and its own cure.
Life is clever.
We are left to dream
for the unseen with no
prediction of the weather.
All of us,
the sheep and the wolves,
within this world together.

All of life
is always in construction;
It's the Creators desire:
love, children, souls,
even the destruction of empires.
And what will future generations
say about us in their time?
Will we be heroes
or will we be cowards…
for how much we loved gold,
but hated each other!
For how much we love freedom,
but had much more love for power.

The Bridge

If you're alive,
then living is here to be explored.
Of yourself, be sure.
And why worry of what you've lost—
It must've never truly been yours.
Some things fall apart
only to come back together.
Such is the story of life,
from now until forever.

Time graces us with
knowledge and understanding
when attention is paid.
So, to Love, the sweet misery,
I will no longer be your slave.

The ferry to our secret island
is no longer in service
and so, we're back on the mainland
with words unspoken and

dreams left within the sand.
Please don't mind me as I leave.
Do what you feel.
Very soon you will understand
mistakes are just tools
to make you a wiser man.
Carpe diem,
I'll be my own treasure.
Don't mind me as I leave
what was never meant to be;
I'd rather make my mind a campground
for large ideas that will last forever.

We are alive
and living is ours to explore.
I have my Father's breath,
I have the lessons that I've felt…
I need nothing more.

So, we meet at the bridge
where we first met.
He wants to keep me
but I want to forget.
He says,
'I can't live without your face.'
I tell him
he'll live.
Let's just have a lovely embrace
within this moment of clarity,
as we forget the lies
and keep the truth,
and keep the bridge—
as it may be of use.

And we'll pop champagne
for the sake of charity,
to remember the jewel
you only loved on Saturdays.

A Broken Thing

I've received naught for my love
but broken things.
Like this lovely heart
that loves to sing.

All the songs have gone and left me…
Left me with a broken tune
with no memory of a melody
and nothing true.
I find myself
lacking in strength.
But I must rise up
from this torment.

It's such sorrow
to behold a singer
who can't sing.
I must put this heart back together,
but where is the glue for such things?

We reach deep for inner strength.
The muscles are there
but they fear too,
and the knees will buckle
as they sometimes do.

We reach even deeper,
and there, within the silence,
is a silent speaker.
Untouchable, complete and blessed.
A small thing
with golden wings
sitting on a treasure chest.

Yes, we must decide
on the side of strength.
If not this,
then what else?

The Climb

I don't know where I'm going.
I feel so stuck.
I feel that I'm feeling nothing,
and this is just not what it once was.
It's the middle of summer,
but I can feel the winter coming…
It's biting.
It's alive and there's no use in running.

Where is the magnanimous sun?
Gone with sweet joy…
both on the run.
Away from me.
Away from here,
where I'm stuck
feeling nothing.

Just sitting pretty
with self-pity.
But then I hear a wise man say

that it never rains every day.
The words taste sweet.
Now I can feel her at my feet.

She reaches for me
as I reach for her.
She has no voice yet,
so, I'll speak for her
and tell sadness that
his time's up.
I can feel her.
I can almost see her
as Hope climbs up.

How Butterflies Fly Away

What were those butterflies last night?
Why do they fly so freely?
How can they be so beautiful?
Do they not know
that life is fleeting?
How unfair is Life,
the giant,
to wrestle with you.
It's a mess here.
A mess hall of infants,
builders, lovers and haters
who all want to mess with you…
all members and spectators
of the great spectacle.

What were those butterflies doing
alive in my dreams?
Flying so high,
so far above the trees?

Oh Sun-shining One,
we see you up there.
Yes, I'm aware:
it was only the sun
that made living
and believing so
easy to bear.

Now on these cloudy days
we must linger through.
What were those butterflies
if not the molecules of you?
You, who we love.
You, who we knew.
Our Sun-shining One,
gone too soon.

Breathing

No one understands
this love of solitude.
No one but the silence and I,
so in love with each other
that we decided
to not bother with the world outside.
Though outside has its good times,
friends, please don't mind me,
as I stay at home with Creativity.
Please forgive me if I seem
anti-social every other day.
It's just the wave,
look how it takes me away.
Yes, look at this skin.
Father made it a temple,
so, I go within.
It pleases this little girl.
It releases me from the
bondage of this mundane world.
This love that I'm in abounds aplenty.

Creativity keeps me alive
even while my tummy is empty…
see, eating is just a distraction.
My lover delights me,
but he thinks I'm part bougie…
My creative appetite is an abstraction
to his psyche,
for how much I love this solitude
and how it uses me.
This love is the most appealing.
It is endless.
It is freeing.
It comes to me as
natural as breathing
air that is fresh.
It is given to me
within each and
every breath.

Self Help

Eventually,
time shows us
a motivation that is
not triggered by joy
nor what is painful.

This motivation
finds you
as it comes through the drive
of opened eyes,
and of being in-tuned
with something inside…

of thriving
and surviving…
of finding the best
that is there within you…
because, if you
think about it,
what else
is there to do?

White Magic and Faith

The hours slip by.
Time is no friend of mine.
He's elusive.
He's intrusive.
He's that annoying voice
that talks too much,
like an old, unmarried hag.
Constantly reminding you
of all the clocks that you have:

Chronological.
Biological.
Planetary,
and all the superficial ones
that varies.

He's a sloth
on your Mondays.
But quickly becomes
Hussein Bolt
on your fun days.

Yay, time chases me
like a rabid dove,
while I chase the knowledge
of self and love.

Time, my warden,
why won't you cooperate?
Why can't you be quiet
and invisible
like white magic and faith?

The Non-Competitor

To say she
didn't play
her cards right
is an understatement,
since she threw away the cards
and replaced them with flowers.
What game of
life is this anyway?
Poker? Spades?
Charades?
It all smells sour.

Or maybe she did know it was a game,
but didn't want to admit it.
Maybe she thought it was a game
with just herself and her eternal spirit.

Or maybe from the start of it
she wanted not one part of it.
Who knows?
Screw it.

We are all born into this game of life
without choice,
long before we had a voice
to object to it.

So, she was forced to play this game
in which she did not desire.
Until a passion was forged
with creative fire.
And now the fire
blazes like a sacred sin,
at its beauty and rules,
and layer of clues given to win.

It's a beautiful song
when you've had ears all along.
It's a wonderful world
but only if you know
how to live and be strong.

We're supposed to keep
our composure
as we compete.
Some are on steroids,
while others have twisted feet.

What a shame,
some players look like
rats in human skin.
While playing this
lovely game of life
the aim is to win.

Win some.
Lose some…
it happens all the time.
Win what you must.
Lose what you must.
Everyone has a different
trophy in mind.

God Body Ascending

True awareness is a gift.
The Creator creates and we,
the Created, salute you
for all that you've built.
We have but one duty, truly,
and that is to be a reflection
of this Divine Beauty.

We're all fallen stardust,
although we can't see it…
Here, putting the puzzle
together, we must.
If it takes a thousand lifetimes,
then so be it.

There is no blasphemy
on a seeker's quest.
There will be no rhapsody
for the flesh.

The only plan
is the ascension of Man's
consciousness,
from an animal
to that of a God Bodied
eye witness.

It is then that
he goes back to
the Source of it all;
back to the oneness
he knew before
the fall.

The Material World

We keep chasing materials
to our doomed allure and lust,
but their world is just a bore.
The only real currency
is of a love so few can afford.

It's all so lovely
when we have eyes.
Yet, how many
people are licensed
but cannot really drive?

The material world
carries a loud call.
But it's just a dream—
it disappears when
to sleep we fall.
Or a fire can quickly take it,
bringing it back to the soil.
Or a broken heart can make it
seem like nothing at all.

Sunny Little Valentines

When the dusk of the day comes,
we'll remember all the fun we had
and all the silly little notions
that made us sad.
It all comes with time.
For now,
you should love yourself and smile.
We're all Sunny Little Valentines.

We're marvelous,
we're fickle.
We're magnificent,
yet, very little
within the vastness of the all.

But with two feet to stand tall,
we were made perfectly.
Oh, how we cannot see
that the all is we,
watered down
and set free,

on Sapphire Blue,
to explore the ideas
of consciousness and truth.

Yes, the all is we,
watered down and set free.
To taste and to feel.
To make the invisible real.

Explorers, we are.
Descendants from stars.
We've come so far.
Look up.
You should love yourself
and smile.
We're all Sunny Little Valentines.

Ode to Self

Love's sweet wine
has taken me to places
that its absence could
never find.

But Magi, oh Priest
please ponder me this:
of how love helps us fly
only to greet the abyss!

From up high,
they smile.
They said:
'it's also love
that helps us climb.'

I look around at my mind.
And, for a time, I was sad.
Until I remembered
all the jewels that I have.

So, I stayed there
a while coasting,
analyzing the breeze
of these emotions.

Yay, how lovely
is Love's sweet wine,
for taking me to places
that its absence
could never find!
And now I can truly see,
that if my heart was broken
for any reason,
it was only to write poetry.

Heaven's Keep

It's summer in India.
The heat is stupendous.
It's hot. So hot, that
the boy feels the sun,
even before *he* comes
to greet his dependents.

Early morning,
the boy stumbled from the
younger prince's palace,
only to then stumble upon
a certain serene madness.

He was the most famous
man in the land—
The Most Wise.
He who left his life of grandness
to meditate and overcome

the sadness of opened eyes.
There he was reflecting,
while pretty flowers sat before
and next to him.

What is this? He thought,
'Maybe I should've went the other way.'
And he thought he heard
a voice that didn't speak say:
'This is where we meet,
all of us, and not missing one,
to greet the rising and setting sun.'
The sun was near the horizon,
so, he would've deemed it to be true.
There was a girl idly watching him
but her lips didn't move.

It was the wine.
Of this he's had plenty.
He looked to his cocoanut shell chalice,
but found it empty.

And then their eyes met.
A rush of blood went to the boy's head
and he knew, the boy knew,
that he would have to defend himself
against those eyes…
Those All-powerful,
All seeing,
All loving eyes.

So, he said:

"The boundaries of the flesh
is an unseen prison,
and we who get high
are only trying to fly.
and be free."

It must have been a gift:
This chance meeting.
An unknown burden lifted
and the boy felt a
spontaneous peace
seep in.

But the Enlightened One
only smiled.
He knew that the boy
would soon realize
a different way into Heaven's Keep:
with the use of one eye,
no hands and no feet...

Better

What a hell of a time.
From the very beginning
he had me under a spell.
He Jodeci wined and dined me…
had me intoxicated well.
He was my Mr. Darcey,
the way his challenges
intrigued and then
assaulted me.
He outshined me
in brilliance
and with magnetism
so resilient,
I was lost
or even blinded
by circumstances
beyond my control.

But how bold of me
to find myself again—
my oldest, most loveliest friend.
I've been warned of this
by all the love songs of my youth—
about the roads of life and how
they aren't often smooth.
But still we move with love,
continuing to
create a better story.
In truth, we all needed our
own point of reference.

And now,
we're all better for it.

Breathe Deep

See how the air
sweetly greets the dove!
Breathe deep, breathe deep
of all that you love.

Because love
is the sweetest thing
that we'll ever know...
Breathe deep, breathe deep
before you have no nose.

List of Illustrations

About the Author

A. Kay Powell is a mixologist living and working in New York City. She fell in love with writing as a child. Also a lover of the natural world, art and history, she is currently working on her debut novel.

Made in United States
North Haven, CT
19 October 2023

42925836R00150